Trigonometry

by

John FK Hoyle

Winner of the
**WriteForTheStage Prize for
New Writing 2016**
Greater Manchester Fringe Festival 2016

CONTENTS

ACKNOWLEDGMENTS

Thanks to Tim and Michael at The Swan. They run the best pub theatre in the area, promoting a massively diverse range of shows, and have been extremely kind to JHC Productions. They premiered our first production *Hardwired* two years ago and have supported us ever since.

Thanks to actress Alice Brockway for bringing both ladies in the script into rich, full life.

Thanks to my lovely family: Jeni, Kacey and Ruby. They have missed me during productions but never complained about me going out at night. I hope they know how much I have missed and love them too.

Thanks to my parents, brothers and aunties who have always supported my shows and continue to turn up and watch.

Thanks to everyone at Playhouse 2, Shaw. They gave me the theatre and continue to be wonderful to me. In particular: Barrie Cottam and Steve & Clare Bennett.

Thanks to the Greater Manchester Fringe for all their support during the run-up to *Trigonometry*, especially Debbie Manley.

Thanks to Nick Payne for good notes on the script and for continuing to be my mate.

Lastly, I am indebted to Hylton Collins. He put on my first show *Answering To The Governor*, has encouraged me to write ever since and *Trigonometry* would simply not have happened without his passion, generosity and willingness to persist with an idea. Thank you so much, mate.

DEDICATION

For Linda.

Trigonometry was first performed Upstairs at The Swan, Dobcross on 26th-July 2016 as part of the Greater Manchester Fringe Festival.

Produced by JHC Productions with the following cast

CHRIS Hylton Collins
TAMMY/SARAH Alice Brockway

Director John FK Hoyle

CHARACTERS
In order of appearance

CHRIS WHITWORTH Mid-forties
TAMMY URQUHART 32
SARAH WHITWORTH Mid-forties

A slash (/) indicates the point when the following speaker begins to overlap.

ORIGINAL PROGRAMME NOTES

Trigonometry was written about 6 years ago and enjoyed a brief uncelebrated life as a rehearsed reading at the 24:7 Theatre Festival under the uninspired title *Happiness and Paranoia*.

Maybe it was the uninspired title which caused this uncelebration?

I changed it. To *Architraves*. Which everybody at The Swan hated. And Hylton who produced this hated. But which I liked.

By committee, I was told to come up with something better. Writers' opinions are worth nothing to anybody, you see? So I shamefacedly changed it to *Jigsaw Without A Picture*. (If *Architraves* had been oblique, then this one was definitely going to get on their wicks!) It remained *Jigsaw Without A Picture* for about eleven minutes before gaining the moniker *Fractured Hearts* (a tad insipid) and then - I thought finally - *Fractures* (even more insipid). For a while I was scared that that might be it. And everybody seemed happy bar me!

The play is about a love triangle. So hoping to reach some form of final, desperate simplicity in my titling endeavour, I suggested, erm... *Triangle*. Hylton pointed out that *Triangle* brought to mind a naked Kate O'Mara on a yacht.

So my brother, Andy, suggested *Trignonometry*. And as always, he crowed about it when I thought it was a good idea. He's still crowing. You can hear him right now over in Royton if you all be quiet for a minute.

I hope you like the play. It's not as complicated as the titling fiasco and hopefully should be more fun. If you don't like the title, blame my brother. I'm washing my hands of it.

John FK Hoyle.

ACT 1 - PROLOGUE

Lights up on **CHRIS**. *A stark lighting - perhaps a red wash or a spot to differentiate it from naturalistic scenes.*

CHRIS There comes a point when you think you've cracked life, that you've got it sorted and everything's more or less pretty much calculable. There aren't very many surprises left really. You know exactly what date your full pension is going to become available and you know you've got 25 years to go before it happens. Until then, you just try to keep hold of your job, keep your head down and try not to upset anyone. Least of all the people you love the most. And if you get promotions along the way then great. And if you manage some pleasant holidays then great. And if anything bad happens you just try and get on with it. Life can be a little bit boring actually. But you never notice it until somebody stops you, usually in a bar, and shows you something a little bit different. A taste of what might have been. What *could* have happened. You just can't legislate for love. It *did* actually start in a bar.

SCENE 1

Bar.

CHRIS *stands with an empty glass.* **TAMMY** *enters, bright, bubbly, a little bit pissed. They have never met.*

TAMMY Hello!

CHRIS *looks at her.*

What?

CHRIS I…erm…

TAMMY Have I got something in my teeth?

CHRIS No, it's…

TAMMY What's with the face then?

CHRIS Huh?

TAMMY *imitates his expression.*

TAMMY Give us a smile, eh?

CHRIS But you're, erm…

TAMMY Yeah?

CHRIS You just…

TAMMY Hmm?

CHRIS No, nothing. It's nothing.

TAMMY OK, well. Shall I say hello again? And you can react like a human being?

CHRIS Are you trying to sell me something, is that it? Have you actually got something to say to me or are you just being bothersome?

TAMMY 'Bothersome?' Is that a word?

CHRIS I believe so.

TAMMY Oh, 'I believe so.' Must be then.

CHRIS You going to stand there and repeat me all night?

TAMMY No, I wouldn't do that. Who you here with?

CHRIS Why? Do you fancy one of my friends?

TAMMY On your own then.

CHRIS Yep.

TAMMY It's not your friends I'm interested in.

CHRIS Look, I appreciate that you've gone for the straight-up option, no flirting. And to be honest, you've made a very good impression. If I were anyone else, I'd be dying to jump into bed with you right now. Fuck it, on the bar. You served yourself up on a silver platter and you were witty and funny and sweetly aggressive. But I happen to be married. Go home.

TAMMY That's the quickest turn down I've ever had.

CHRIS Well, that's not surprising; you're very pretty. But I'm sure you're aware of that.

TAMMY Definitely not interested?

CHRIS I'm married.

TAMMY Is that a no?

CHRIS I'm married.

TAMMY Still not a no.

CHRIS What?

TAMMY At least let me buy you a drink. To apologise, yeah?

CHRIS Suits me. If you've got it to burn.

TAMMY What'll it be?

CHRIS Whisky.

TAMMY Hardcore.

CHRIS Hmm.

TAMMY (*To imaginary barman*) Double whisky. On the rocks. On the rocks?

CHRIS On the rocks.

TAMMY On the rocks. Good oh. And I'll have a white wine and soda please. With ice. Yeah, I can *see* you're very busy. Whenever. (*To Chris*) The attitude of some people! What's your name?

CHRIS Chris.

TAMMY Ah, boring name.

CHRIS What's yours?

TAMMY Tammy.

CHRIS Short for Tamzin?

TAMMY Ah, don't say it.

CHRIS You don't like it?

TAMMY I've got a shit name; you've got a boring name. Result.

CHRIS Tamzin's nice.

TAMMY It's shit. Give over.

Pause.

CHRIS I'm not gonna sleep with you.

TAMMY I'm not asking you to.

CHRIS Don't you think you should be getting back to your friends?

TAMMY What friends?

CHRIS You're here on your own too?

TAMMY As always.

CHRIS Oh. Why?

TAMMY What do you mean?

CHRIS Well, look at you. Young. What are you, 36?

TAMMY 32, thanks.

CHRIS In a bar. On your own. What's that about?

TAMMY There are a lot of very good looking older men in here. With lots of money and a sex drive their wives can't satisfy.

Pause. Realisation.

CHRIS Listen, you're not…

TAMMY No, sorry, it's not…

CHRIS Just cos… You're not…

TAMMY No, it's OK, it's OK. I'm not/on the job

CHRIS …on the job.

Pause.

Just, was gonna… (*He indicates with a thumb over the shoulder that he was going to scarper.*)

TAMMY It's alright. Just meant… I like older men. That's all. Don't have to put up with all the angst.

CHRIS Well, this older man is not for you.

Pause. She sizes him up, then:

TAMMY Right. I've obviously got the wrong idea. Forget it. You're a married man. Very happy. I understand. I've already proven I can't chat up a bloke for toffee and I obviously look like a prostitute. I can see how it'd be easy to be turned off by… that.

CHRIS It's OK.

TAMMY Thanks.

CHRIS See you.

TAMMY Yep.

Long pause.

CHRIS Well are you going or what?

TAMMY I'm on my own.

CHRIS Oh God.

TAMMY You're not a perv and you're fairly intelligent. Can I stay here for a bit?

CHRIS It's a free country. How do you know I'm intelligent?

TAMMY Your bearing.

CHRIS My bearing?

TAMMY Yeah, your bearing. You look fairly intelligent.

CHRIS I'm not.

TAMMY Only clever people think that.

Pause.

CHRIS (*Reluctant*) What do you do, Tammy?

TAMMY I work for a very posh travel agency.

CHRIS You've seen the world?

TAMMY No, I just work in their office. Pay packet's pretty amazing. I'm not complaining. You?

CHRIS Building company.

TAMMY Out and about with your hands?

CHRIS No. I sit in their office. Well, my office. Pay packet's pretty amazing.

TAMMY Ooh, I like a man with money.

CHRIS Funny that. Women with money irritate me.

TAMMY Come off it. Double whisky; no questions.

CHRIS I suppose so.

TAMMY And I don't spend it all on shoes and underwear and the things you probably imagine I spend it on.

CHRIS What do you imagine I imagine you'd spend it on?

TAMMY The aforementioned.

CHRIS What do you spend it on?

TAMMY (*Embarrassed but stolid*) Ornaments. I buy ornaments. I love ornaments. I spend all my money on ornaments. The house is a shit tip but in it… it's got a lot o' lovely ornaments.

CHRIS Heaven… if you *like* ornaments.

TAMMY What do you spend yours on?

CHRIS My wife.

TAMMY (*Begrudgingly*) OK.

CHRIS It's not happening. Sorry. You're wasting your time. Give the drink to someone else. I'm off.

He goes to leave.

TAMMY I need a builder.

CHRIS I'm off duty.

TAMMY I can pay a lot of money. I'm guessing you're on commission, builder who sits in his office all day.

Pause.

CHRIS You've got two minutes.

TAMMY I need my banisters fixing. My house is a new-build and the banisters are shitty. They're falling off.

CHRIS This is work.

TAMMY This is work.

CHRIS How many staircases have you got?

Pause.

TAMMY One.

CHRIS OK. Not a big enough job. We don't really go in for...

TAMMY Oh, please, Chris. I don't... I don't know anybody.

CHRIS First name terms already, Christ. I'm not sending people round to fix the banisters for you. We build houses. We don't fix staircases. I'm sorry.

TAMMY I'll have a whole new staircase put in.

CHRIS Are you that desperate?

TAMMY Desperate must be the word... looking at you.

CHRIS Here's my card. Phone me in the morning if you still want a new staircase. But when you wake up, I imagine you'll wonder what sort of drugs you were on last night that had you chatting up some old guy with whisky breath and a rubbish beard. I'm going. Nice to meet you, Tamzin. If that drink does ever turn up, have it.

TAMMY If that's what you want.

Blackout.

SCENE 2

TAMMY's staircase.

CHRIS Yep. That's a mess alright.

TAMMY I'm not stupid.

CHRIS I can't believe you let 'em leave the house.

TAMMY Neither can I. Five sexy builders. Now how much is it gonna cost me to have it fixed?

CHRIS Well, it's probably the steel frame in your banisters which is twisted. That's why the wood's all to fuck. Sorry, pardon my French.

TAMMY Say whatever you like. I'm not proud.

CHRIS It'll be a new-build. From scratch. What I'm saying, basically, is...

TAMMY Ah-ah. Anyone who starts on with 'basically' is usually about to tell me a big, long, rambling story. I just want a price.

CHRIS You're looking at around a grand.

TAMMY How much is it gonna be, Chris?

CHRIS Realistically, 14 to 15 hundred quid. The lads'll try to rip me off. That's all I'll give 'em. Won't be more than 15, I promise.

TAMMY You're a shit salesman. The last lot charged me two grand and I thought it was a bargain. Why didn't you ask me how much they'd charged then up it a bit? And d'you know? I still don't trust you. 15 hundred, my arse.

CHRIS Do you want your banisters doing or don't you?

TAMMY Yes, yes, yes! Sorry. 15 hundred's fine.

Pause.

Thanks. For coming, you know. I didn't think you would.

CHRIS This is work.

TAMMY I know! (*Changing the subject*) Were you surprised?

CHRIS Sorry?

TAMMY That I called?

CHRIS Not bothered. It's work, right?

TAMMY If you say so.

CHRIS No, it is. I'm here to look over this.

TAMMY How much are the jobs you usually price up?

CHRIS Beg your pardon?

TAMMY Well, this is 15 hundred quid. What's the usual sort of price for one of your jobs?

CHRIS Well, it varies…

TAMMY Average, Chris. Give me an average.

CHRIS Every job's different. It could be anything from…

TAMMY Try to get a straight answer from a builder! Average job.

CHRIS Probably… the builds we do… between 50 and 75 grand. Usually. Sometimes higher. We regularly do jobs over 150 k, all told. We did one last year 400 thousand. Part of an estate.

TAMMY Impressive.

CHRIS Hmm.

Pause.

TAMMY So what you fucking about with a staircase for?

CHRIS I told you one staircase was unusual.

TAMMY Why are you doing it then?

CHRIS A favour.

TAMMY And what are you gonna tell your boss?

CHRIS There's only four of us. It's for a friend. We do it all the time. It's still money.

TAMMY But you hardly know me.

CHRIS Well, you asked.

TAMMY And this is definitely work, right?

CHRIS Yeah.

TAMMY Bollocks.

Pause.

CHRIS Well, if I'm done, I'll be off.

TAMMY No way. I've been sat in all day waiting for you to turn up. Why do people like you always give out ridiculous appointment times? 'Sometime between 12 and 6,' your secretary said!

CHRIS Molly's way of never letting anyone down.

TAMMY But it means I've been here hours waiting and you rock up at 3 o'clock without so much as a 'Sorry I'm late.' No, you stay and let me waste a bit of your time.

CHRIS God, you're hard work. What's the point, Tammy?

TAMMY I'm lonely.

Pause.

CHRIS Ten minutes. Then I need to go back to the office.

TAMMY Wa-hey!

CHRIS I'm not playing your games though.

TAMMY Chill out, Christopher. I won't force you to do anything you don't wanna do.

CHRIS Christ, what are you on?

TAMMY You're my guest! Relax!

CHRIS I'm a man from the building company. That's all.

TAMMY In my house, boy. Watch your mouth. Can I get you a drink?

Pause.

CHRIS You got any lemonade?

TAMMY No. As it happens. Are you being awkward?

CHRIS No. Sorry. Just fancied a lemonade.

TAMMY Well I'm going to have a beer like any normal person. A day off work. Friday afternoon. Sun's shining. Suit yourself though Mr Lemonade Eccentric.

CHRIS Go on then. If you really insist, I'll have a beer.

TAMMY You're pathetic, you.

She exits to get drinks.

CHRIS Listen… I need to tell you something.

TAMMY (*Off*) What?

Pause.

CHRIS 'S a bit weird.

TAMMY (*Off*) What?

CHRIS You look…?

TAMMY (*Off*) I look…?

CHRIS You just look…

TAMMY (*Off*) Yeah?

CHRIS Doesn't matter.

Blackout.

SCENE 3

TAMMY's living room.

CHRIS *is tucking his shirt in and buckling up his belt.*

TAMMY Chris, would you stop?!

CHRIS No. Shit. Sorry, Tammy. No, I'm going. I've got to…

TAMMY It's only shock. Just calm down, Chris.

CHRIS You tell me to, you tell me to calm down, after, after…

TAMMY It's OK. It's alright. Don't panic. I'm not gonna tell anybody.

CHRIS It's not that.

TAMMY Why are you so uppity then? Bouncing about like a fucking rabbit.

CHRIS Are you trying to be funny?

TAMMY Oh. Right. Rabbits. Yeah. Shit. Sorry. *Bad* choice of metaphor.

CHRIS I'm not laughing, Tammy. I can't believe, I can't, I can't believe I've… (*Lets out a deep breath.*) I've got to go. My wife. It's, I'm sorry, I won't…

TAMMY Sit down, Chris. Your flies are still undone.

Embarrassed and silenced, **CHRIS** *sits down. Pause.*

CHRIS Let me get my act together. Then I'm going.

TAMMY It's your life. Just don't go anywhere in this state. Anyone'd think you were gonna throw yourself off a bridge, gimbling and gurning and being all expressive. You look like a rubbish mime artist.

CHRIS (*Succumbs, laughs but stifles it*) Sorry. I'm just... (*Then louder, angry again*) I just can't bloody think.

TAMMY It's OK. It's OK. I'll put the kettle on. Cup of tea. You'll be fine.

CHRIS I've never, erm, I don't do this...

TAMMY I know you don't. Don't panic. It happens. All the time. Just men. Forget it.

CHRIS I don't want to be 'just men.'

TAMMY Let me get you a cup of tea.

CHRIS OK. Ta.

TAMMY *goes.* **CHRIS** *sits a minute. Shaking slightly. Hands between his legs.*

And it's a simile! Not a metaphor! *Like* a fucking rabbit is a simile!

Slowly, his breathing returns to normal.

Oh. Shit. Chris.

TAMMY *returns.*

TAMMY Kettle's on. Do you have milk and sugar?

CHRIS Just milk thanks. Not too much.

TAMMY Not too much milk. Fine.

She comes to sit with him.

TAMMY You calmed down yet?

CHRIS Yeah. I'm sorry.

TAMMY It's like you've been in a car accident. You know how people are when they're in shock afterwards? All shaky and rambling bollocks.

CHRIS Great. You think I'm weird.

TAMMY I don't. I think… you've not done this before.

CHRIS No.

Pause.

Is this what your men are usually like?

TAMMY Men?

CHRIS From the pub. Your rich men whose wives can't make them come. Is this how they usually react?

TAMMY This is not habitual.

CHRIS Come off it. What were you like when I first met you?

TAMMY I was only acting.

CHRIS Well, you had me fooled. You ought to be in films.

TAMMY Ooh, no. Not for me thanks.

CHRIS So what did you see in me, eh?

TAMMY You're fishing for compliments. Trying to make yourself feel better. They aren't coming.

Pause.

You're more than welcome to… stay here./I mean if you want to. If it's easier. But there's no obligation. Just… Not like I haven't got room.

CHRIS No. No. I won't be… I didn't want to… in the first place. It just… happened. I wasn't thinking that I, it was… I'm not sure that I should… I shouldn't.

TAMMY It's alright. I know you lot. You don't have to make excuses.

CHRIS I'll shut up. Only saying. I won't be staying here. I need to get back. She'll be missing me.

TAMMY Your wife?

CHRIS Don't mention her please.

TAMMY Sorry?

CHRIS Sorry, this is just too weird.

TAMMY OK.

Pause.

It's alright. You don't have to protect her from this any more than you can by simply not telling her.

CHRIS Are you just being heartless or are you analysing what I'm doing? This last half hour you've done nothing but bloody analyse me. 'That'll be the shock, that'll be your first time nerves.' I'm not a case study. So stop it. Stop analysing me. Stop. I feel like I'm in a fucking zoo.

TAMMY Analysing stops as of now.

CHRIS And stop being nice! You're like one of those irritating psycho-analysts on American telly. They're having a breakdown in front of you and you're being eternally calm about it! Calm isn't contagious, you know! In fact, a man who *isn't* calm is only going to be deeply *irked* by someone, a woman in particular, being stupidly calm. It's only gonna make him less calm. Not more calm. God, I want to shake you! Would you stop being so fucking calm!

TAMMY Why do I get the impression I'm dealing with this a little bit better than you?

CHRIS (*Deflated*) You win. Have it your way. I'm calm.

TAMMY There we are. Back with us. I'm glad you've got a sense of humour.

CHRIS I don't think I want that brew.

TAMMY Do you know how much electricity you use boiling a kettle?

CHRIS I don't want it.

TAMMY It's OK.

Pause.

You driving home or have you had too much?

CHRIS I'm not driving like this.

TAMMY Do you need money for a taxi?

CHRIS I'm walking anyway.

TAMMY It's miles, isn't it?

CHRIS Might do me good. Nice long walk. Clear my head a bit.

TAMMY It's pissing down.

CHRIS It's only raining. As per. Why do people complain about the rain? We live in England. Capital of Rain. It rains every other day. Do people spend 50% of their lives complaining about fucking weather? We can't change it, so just get on with it. We'll have evolved webbed feet in 20 years then we can all shut up about it for good. Probably be dead by then so I won't be around to enjoy that day. Such is life.

TAMMY (*Laughing*) Well, if you get that worked up about a bit of rain then you'll definitely be dead. 5 years, heart attack. Gone.

CHRIS Why do I give myself 20 years and you only give me 5?

TAMMY Old man.

Pause.

CHRIS I'm really sorry.

TAMMY What for?

CHRIS Being so mental.

TAMMY It's not your fault. Can't help how you feel. To be honest, I'd rather you didn't pretend. At least I know where I am with you.

CHRIS I don't want you to think that I promised you anything. I don't want to have let you down.

TAMMY I had a good night! It was fun.

CHRIS OK then.

TAMMY It was really good.

CHRIS Yeah.

Pause.

TAMMY It's a shame really. I mean… no, it doesn't matter.

CHRIS What?

TAMMY No, it's not fair.

CHRIS What?

TAMMY Forget it.

CHRIS Do I have to ask you again?

TAMMY I had a *really* good night.

Pause.

CHRIS I can't. I can't, Tammy. I can't do it to her.

TAMMY OK.

Pause.

Finally meet someone you like, who's… it's *exciting* and… And he's married.

CHRIS Right, well… Yeah. I'd, err… better go. Sorry for being so… brief and… shit, but…

TAMMY It's alright. Go.

CHRIS I'll ring you, Tammy. About work. I know the stairs need…

TAMMY I'm here if you want me.

CHRIS Thanks, Tammy. I'll…I'll see you…

Blackout.

SCENE 4

Restaurant. Table, vase.

CHRIS *has been here a while.* **TAMMY** *is just sitting down.*

TAMMY Well, this is… unexpected.

CHRIS It wasn't planned.

TAMMY Course it was. You invited me. You planned it yourself.

CHRIS No, I mean I wasn't... it wasn't the big plan to… to get you coming to restaurants or… what I'm saying is…this isn't, well, you know… a date. I just, how can I put…?… I had to just tell you some things.

TAMMY Well if it's going to take as long as that glorious opening speech it can wait. I've only just sat down. What are we drinking?

CHRIS Erm, oh, err, pint of bitter.

TAMMY In this restaurant?

CHRIS What?

TAMMY It's a bit posh for bitter, this place.

CHRIS So? I'm a real man, me. I drink what I want, where I want.

TAMMY Bitter it is then, real man. I'll have a white wine and soda please. With lots of ice. In the biggest glass they've got. Not the house. It's always shit.

CHRIS What's the point in getting an expensive wine if you're gonna dilute it?

TAMMY That's what I want.

CHRIS Fine. The cheapest and most expensive drinks in the place. I suppose the bill'll end up somewhere in the middle.

TAMMY Have you looked at the menu?

CHRIS You were late. Course I have.

TAMMY And?

CHRIS Salmon I think.

TAMMY With bitter?

CHRIS I like salmon. I like bitter. What's the problem?

TAMMY Together?

CHRIS Look, stop picking holes would you?

TAMMY I'll have the trout. Don't want to step on your toes by going for salmon too.

CHRIS Just have the same. What's it matter?

TAMMY Two plates of the same meal on the same table is just wrong.

CHRIS Right. *I'll* have the trout. You have the salmon.

TAMMY Thank you!

CHRIS 'S fine.

Pause. A moment.

You look nice.

TAMMY There it is. Thanks. You don't. You might have shaved.

CHRIS Thought you liked a bit of rough.

TAMMY Ha!

CHRIS No?

TAMMY You?

CHRIS What?

TAMMY Bit of rough?

CHRIS Am I not?

TAMMY Hardly. Mr Builder Who Wears A Suit To Work.

CHRIS Why do you always have to talk about jobs and pay and salaries?

TAMMY You've spent the night so far talking about the bill!

CHRIS But talking salaries is vulgar.

TAMMY Thought you liked a bit of vulgar.

CHRIS Please don't.

Pause.

TAMMY Right. Go on then. What's up? I know you've been dying to tell me what the problem is.

CHRIS Why, what's...?

TAMMY Just tell me what you want to tell me. Maybe we can leave early.

CHRIS What?

TAMMY Please tell me.

CHRIS Now?

TAMMY Now. I can't bear anticipation.

Pause.

CHRIS It's your joiners.

TAMMY My joiners?

CHRIS We've cancelled our contract with them. So they can't come next week. Sorry. You'll have to wait, probably a fortnight, before we can get the new guys in. Formalities, all that. Maybe longer. Sorry.

TAMMY S'alright. Forget it.

CHRIS Sorry.

TAMMY You said.

CHRIS I mean you can sue us if you like. We've put funds aside for that. They've fucked up so many bleeding jobs.

TAMMY Fine.

Pause.

Fucking waiters. How come when you come to a swanky place, the service is always shit and when they eventually get to you they act as if you've just crapped on the table?

CHRIS Sorry. I'll try to flag him down next time he comes past.

Pause.

Do you eat out very much?

TAMMY I would if I had someone to go out with. Not coming to places like this on my own, though. No way. They can kiss my arse.

CHRIS (*Laughs, then genuinely appreciative*) You're so... wonderfully crass.

TAMMY What? Just saying.

CHRIS Honest crass. I like it.

TAMMY You couldn't be honest if you tried. And there's another thing you do that pisses me off.

CHRIS I pay you a compliment; you pick holes again. How does this work?

TAMMY I don't do compliments. What's the point in telling people what they already know? If they're making mistakes, they're obviously unaware. I'm actually very helpful.

CHRIS You don't believe what you just said. You just liked the sound of it.

TAMMY Yeah?

CHRIS Yeah… What's this other thing then?

TAMMY Beg your pardon?

CHRIS That pisses you off?

TAMMY You apologise too much.

CHRIS Sorry.

TAMMY And again!

CHRIS Yeah.

Pause.

TAMMY (*Pointedly*) So that's it, is it? Joiners? It's all about the joiners.

CHRIS I don't catch your drift.

TAMMY You've brought me to a restaurant to apologise for your rubbish joiners? You could have done that over the phone.

CHRIS I wanted to apologise. In person.

TAMMY Yeah right.

CHRIS I wanted to apologise.

TAMMY With an expensive wine and a trout special?

CHRIS This is my job. Customer relations. We want you to use us again.

TAMMY You just told me you wouldn't mind if I sued you! Your bosses'd have a field day with you. Why am I here, Chris?

CHRIS So I could tell you what was what. And say sorry. As an ambassador/ for the company.

TAMMY Alright. Forget work. Forget your ambassadorial role. Put our professional relationship in that vase for a minute and forget it's there. Why am I here?

CHRIS For me to apologise to you.

TAMMY Professional life in the vase!

CHRIS I wanted to…

TAMMY In the vase!

CHRIS I just wanted to buy you dinner!

Pause.

TAMMY God, that took long enough. Christ, I'm worn out now.

CHRIS I wanted to buy you dinner and have a nice evening.

TAMMY Nothing mysterious or clandestine about the/ whole thing?

CHRIS And to tell you that… our night… you know, the night, we…

TAMMY Yep.

CHRIS Well, it can't happen again.

Pause.

TAMMY OK. Well, I suppose it was about time we had this talk...You've been avoiding contacting me for a week.

CHRIS I'm sorry. I don't want to just... I mean, I want to explain myself. I've been thinking about this for ages, it's not...I've had some time. I've had some time to...

TAMMY Deep breaths. I fear I'm not going to like this but go on. I'll stay calm if you do.

CHRIS I just can't do it to my wife.

TAMMY (*Pointedly*) What's she doing tonight?

CHRIS Fuck off. I love my wife. Things might be difficult right now but...

Pause.

TAMMY You think you're so romantic don't you? You think you can make this into a love story?

CHRIS I love my wife, Tammy.

TAMMY Love her enough to sleep with me?

CHRIS Just don't mention her, OK?!

TAMMY Do you want to kiss me yet?

Pause.

Come on. I know what's going on. I'm not a fucking idiot.

CHRIS I needed to see you again.

TAMMY Remind yourself how ordinary-looking I am?

CHRIS No.

TAMMY Convince yourself you could avoid me? That you didn't need me for anything?

CHRIS Sort of.

TAMMY What?

CHRIS I just really needed to see you.

Pause.

TAMMY No, I'm not playing. Sorry. I hoped it'd be good news. I knew it wouldn't be. I can't be arsed with you. You're bloody weird and you're soft as horse shit.

CHRIS Tamzin.

TAMMY Tammy.

CHRIS But I love Tamzin.

TAMMY Freudian slip?

CHRIS I meant the name. You've got a wonderful name.

TAMMY I hate it. Tammy: That's better. Sounds like a cat.

Pause.

CHRIS Can I see you again? One more time?

Pause.

TAMMY You've known me a month. You phone me. You sleep with me. You shit yourself. Your whole world's tumbling down. Mid-life crisis all over it.

CHRIS My head's screwed on properly. I just… kept thinking about you… (*Shyly*) About your body.

TAMMY Oh it's my body now, is it? Shall I send you some pictures?

CHRIS No, no, no, it's not that.

TAMMY Chris, I've had enough. I thought tonight might be a laugh. Bit of a giggle. But you don't know what you want, who you want, or how to get either. You've told me it's over, that you love me and that you're not getting on with your wife in all of five minutes and I'm buggered if I'm going to listen to the next meaningless, meandering, gobshite to drip off the end of your mouth. So let me go home. The waiter's obviously not coming and I'm getting hungry for trout.

CHRIS Wait, no, please…

TAMMY Please don't.

CHRIS Tamzin.

TAMMY Don't. And it's Tammy. And she's going home. Goodnight.

She leaves.

Blackout.

SCENE 5

CHRIS's living room. **CHRIS** *enters through the front door. That same night. It's late.*

CHRIS (*His voice has a soft delicacy to it*) Sarah? Sarah, I'm back. Are you up? Sorry, it's late. Steven got carried away. You should have seen him. Had to virtually drag him into a taxi. I don't know how he gets like that so quickly. Maybe Helen doesn't let him drink any other time. Stone cold sober at home, so when he goes out...

SARAH *enters. She is wheelchair bound and suffers from multiple sclerosis. Her back is arched so that her hair dangles in front of her face. We never see it so we're reliant on SARAH's voice. Her hands are gnarled but she can just about operate the chair. Her speech is perfectly fine. She is played by the same actor as* **TAMMY**.

CHRIS Hello love.

SARAH Had a nice time?

CHRIS It was alright. Did Tim pop in to make you a brew?

SARAH Yeah, about half past seven.

CHRIS Good. You look well today.

SARAH Give over.

CHRIS You do. You look better than last week.

SARAH Ah well. There's something, eh?

CHRIS Do you want anything? Are you hungry? Do you want telly on?

SARAH No. There's never anything on after ten. I'll have one of those cup o' soups, though, if you don't mind.

CHRIS Course I don't mind. Give me a sec.

CHRIS *exits into the kitchen.* **SARAH** *is alone a moment.*

CHRIS It's boiling.

CHRIS *comes in and sits next to her. Pause.*

CHRIS You OK?

Pause.

SARAH I erm… I had an accident again today.

CHRIS Oh no.

SARAH It's alright. Tim sorted it.

CHRIS Do I have to ask Doctor Isaacs to come round to see you again?

SARAH No, no. It's only the second time. And it's been months since the first one. I should be fine.

CHRIS I don't want you worrying though, Sarah. If you're worried let me know. I'll get Doctor Isaacs round. He'll put your mind at ease.

SARAH You always talk about me being worried.

CHRIS Sorry?

SARAH Never you.

CHRIS Hmm?

Pause.

SARAH Do you never worry?

CHRIS I don't understand you.

SARAH Are you never worried about me?

CHRIS (*Genuinely*) My worries can be kept to myself. They needn't bother you, Sarah.

SARAH You do then?

CHRIS Course I do.

Pause.

SARAH Go and look in the kitchen cupboard.

CHRIS Hmm?

SARAH The one next to the fridge. Go on. Go and look.

CHRIS Something's going on. What are you playing at?

SARAH Go and see.

CHRIS *exits. Then, from the kitchen*

CHRIS (*Off*) No way!

SARAH Is it the one you wanted?

CHRIS *comes back in, clutching a red, hardback book.*

CHRIS Yes, it's gorgeous! Oh, Sarah! Where, where did you...?

SARAH eBay. Tim and I sat bidding on it for an hour last week. Came through the letterbox today.

CHRIS Look at the binding, the... oh, it's a glorious, glorious thing.

SARAH Is that the lot now?

CHRIS That's the lot. Thank you.

He goes to kneel at the bottom of her chair so that she can see his face. He clutches the book hard.

Thank you so much, Sarah. This is... wonderful.

SARAH I knew you'd like it.

CHRIS *stifles an involuntary, sudden sob.*

Oh, what is it, Chris?

CHRIS Nothing, nothing. Sorry. Just happy. Just...

SARAH Is it beer?

CHRIS Yeah. Well, must be. It's...

SARAH Don't worry. Shush. I don't like to hear you crying.

CHRIS I'm not crying. I'm OK. *You* shush.

SARAH You always used to tell me to shush.

CHRIS Shush again. You'll set me off. I'm happy.

SARAH Sorry.

Pause.

CHRIS 15 years I've been collecting these.

SARAH I know. And now you can stop, can't you?

CHRIS What will I do with my life?

SARAH Will you spontaneously combust?

CHRIS *smiles up at her. Stillness.*

CHRIS I love you, Sarah.

SARAH Love you too.

CHRIS Don't just say it... as a response... I want... I want you to mean it.

SARAH Of course I mean it!

CHRIS Well think about it before you say it then, will you? I want to feel all your love through those words.

SARAH Do you not?

CHRIS Not when it's just a robotic reply.

SARAH It's never *just* a reply. I do happen to love you, you know. Nothing's changed since we got married. I loved you then and I love you now and that's the end of it. If there doesn't seem to be any emotion in my voice it's because that fact has become a part of my life. Something I just know.

Like the sky is blue. Day follows night. Trains go fast. I love Chris Whitworth.

CHRIS Good.

SARAH Hmm. You don't sound too convinced.

CHRIS I am.

Pause.

You realise I'll have to start collecting something else now?

SARAH Oh dear.

CHRIS Was thinking comics.

SARAH Ooh, no.

CHRIS Bit of Spiderman, bit of The Hulk. You'll love it. You can read 'em when I'm finished but don't be getting your greasy paw prints all over the pages.

SARAH Geek.

CHRIS I know.

Pause.

Do *you* need anything to read?

SARAH No. There are still a couple I've got to finish.

CHRIS OK.

SARAH The radio needs tuning though. I couldn't be graceful enough with it.

CHRIS I'll do it in the morning. Fuck it, I'll programme the remote so you can hop channels. Should have done that ages ago. Sorry.

SARAH Thanks.

Pause.

I missed you tonight.

CHRIS Oh, Sarah.

SARAH I know, I know I'm being selfish. I know I am. I just... missed you.

CHRIS I've got to go out sometimes, Sarah. I realise it must be awful for you... these four walls. On your own. But I've got to...

SARAH Sorry, it's me. It's me. I'm being selfish. You deserve a night out. Every now and again, you must. You must go out.

CHRIS Sorry, Sarah.

SARAH Don't be. It's me. I'm getting paranoid. Not getting out of the house much, eh? Anyway... it's only Steven.

Long pause.

Don't worry, Chris.

CHRIS I'm not.

SARAH I know when you're worrying. All the signs. The little pauses.

CHRIS I'm not worrying. You're imagining things.

SARAH Don't worry. That's all I'm saying.

CHRIS What do *I* have to worry about, Sarah?

SARAH I don't know.

CHRIS I'm not worried.

Pause.

SARAH Think I just heard the kettle click.

CHRIS I'm not worried.

Pause.

SARAH In fact, sorry, I'm a bit tired.

CHRIS You don't want any soup now?

SARAH You have it. You must be hungry. It's late.

CHRIS You want to go to bed?

SARAH I'm tired.

CHRIS Shall I take you to bed?

SARAH Sorry, Chris.

CHRIS It's OK. I'm just getting ratty. Yeah, course I'll take you to bed.

SARAH Sorry. I was saying I missed you, and then I'm saying I want to sleep, and you must…

CHRIS It's late. I'll take you to bed. I'll come and get in… in a little while.

SARAH OK.

Pause.

CHRIS In fact, I'm not gonna sleep tonight. I hate drinking too much. If you'd rather, I can kip on the settee.

SARAH No, come to bed in a bit. Put your arms round my tummy. I like it when you do that. When I can feel your breath on my neck.

CHRIS OK.

Pause.

Do you want to go then?

SARAH Yeah.

He wheels her towards the exit.

CHRIS Come on then, you.

He uses his foot to open the door. And they go out.

Blackout.

Lights up on **CHRIS** *as in* PROLOGUE.

CHRIS I thought I'd put it all to bed. That it was something really bad I'd done but that in time I could forget it had ever happened. And I could carry on chugging along at a steady, even pace. And think only of Sarah. Forever. But it didn't work like that.

ACT 2 SCENE 1

CHRIS's office.

CHRIS *is working. Lots of documents at his desk. Some time later. His buzzer goes. He answers.*

CHRIS Yeah.

MOLLY (*V/O*) There's a Tamzin Urquhart here, Chris. Says she's got an appointment with you but she's not in my diary. Are you due to see her?

Pause.

(*V/O*) Chris?

CHRIS Yeah. Send her in.

CHRIS *clears his desk. Enter* **TAMMY**.

This is where I work. What are you doing here?

TAMMY I had to. Sorry. I had to come and see you.

CHRIS What? Why? It's been weeks. Are you…? This is where I work!

TAMMY I know. I'm sorry. But. I had to see you.

CHRIS What for? We finished everything didn't we? Well, you did.

TAMMY I'm sorry, sorry. That's what I came to say, that I'm sorry.

CHRIS Shall I say it again? This is where I work.

TAMMY Right. So I knew you'd be here.

CHRIS I could have been with a customer. I could have been on site. What..?

TAMMY Just coincidence. Spotted your car. Thought your secretary'd turn me away if you were indisposed.

CHRIS Molly's nice but not the brightest spark. She'd have sent you in anyway. Your stairs are fixed, aren't they? Don't tell me you've had more problems cos this lot have been/ just as...

TAMMY My stairs are fine. Thank you. For arranging everything so quickly. Even if you wouldn't speak to me directly.

CHRIS I thought one of the apprentices could handle it. Tiny job like that.

Long pause.

TAMMY I'm here cos I missed you. Sorry for being horrible with you in the restaurant.

CHRIS It's fine. But Tammy...

TAMMY What?

Pause.

CHRIS (*Bravely, disingenuous*) I stopped missing you a while ago. It was a fad. It was a ... just a panic I was in. I don't... want you anymore. Sorry.

Pause.

TAMMY I saw you in town yesterday.

CHRIS And?

TAMMY You were with your wife.

Pause.

I'm sorry.

Pause.

It just all clicked. I understand now. How angry you were. And… I wish you'd told me. Cos…

CHRIS Told you what?

TAMMY About how she is.

CHRIS It doesn't matter how she is and I don't think it's any of your business.

TAMMY So… it was… I was just… I was just sex?

CHRIS Yep. Sorry.

Pause.

TAMMY (*Unsure*) Do you want some more just sex?

CHRIS No!

Pause.

TAMMY (*Embarrassed*) I shouldn't be here. I'm really sorry. I'm wasting my time. I'll go.

CHRIS No, wait a bit. If you go now, Molly'll be suspicious. And she's a nosey cow.

TAMMY Oh thanks. This isn't going to be awkward at all.

CHRIS Sorry. That's how it is.

Long pause.

So you came here to ask me out, did you?

TAMMY I felt sorry for you.

CHRIS Don't. It was my decision. I knew she'd get worse when I married her. I stood in a church and I vowed to look after her. And I will.

TAMMY OK… If I'd known…

CHRIS What? If you'd known she were disabled, you'd have done things differently, would you?

TAMMY No, I'd have just… understood you a bit better. Your moods, your…

CHRIS Well, I'm not around to be understood anymore. I told you to stop trying to fucking analyse me.

Pause.

TAMMY How long has she been like that?

CHRIS She's been getting tireder and tireder for six years. Last year, I couldn't see her face anymore.

TAMMY Is she OK?

CHRIS No, she's not OK. She stares into her knees all day. She's got an adjustable armchair, helps her lean up to the sky to be able to fucking read.

TAMMY I'm so sorry.

She puts her hand on his arm. He instantly relaxes.

CHRIS Can we not talk about her anymore, please?

Long pause.

Everything goes through Molly's diary. Everything.

TAMMY Oh?

CHRIS She'll be suspicious anyway.

TAMMY Right?

CHRIS *looks at her. A long time.* **TAMMY** *smiles gently.* **CHRIS** *kisses her passionately. Then pulls himself away suddenly.*

CHRIS Please leave me alone.

TAMMY What?

CHRIS Go. Go. Go.

TAMMY Chris?!

CHRIS Just get out. I've had it up to here with you.

TAMMY *(Bitter)* Course you have.

He turns from her to his desk, leans on it.

CHRIS Please just leave me alone.

Pause.

TAMMY (*Attitude*) OK.

TAMMY *leaves.* **CHRIS** *kicks his desk. A moment.*

MOLLY (*V/O*) Is everything alright in there, Chris?

CHRIS Yeah. Just. Never mind Molly. It's…

Blackout.

SCENE 2

CHRIS's living room.

The same day.

CHRIS *is pacing.* **SARAH** *sits in the wheelchair stock still.*

CHRIS Three customers today. All with problems. I've been chasing people around all day.

SARAH What was wrong?

CHRIS Architraves. Bleeding architraves. One feller wasn't happy with his architraves. How can you mess up architraves? So I sent Neil round to look at 'em and he said they were a botched job which means I'm gonna have to get the joiners in again, and they'll want paying again, so that'll be another five hundred quid on expenses. I'm gonna cancel the contract with those joiners. They've given us nothing but trouble. Joiners are all shit. Am I boring you? This is boring.

SARAH No, I like hearing your voice.

CHRIS Well, I'm boring myself so I'd better stop before I get angry.

SARAH OK, we can talk about something else.

Pause.

CHRIS What've you been up to?

SARAH Finished that book you bought for me.

CHRIS Any good?

SARAH Tolerable.

CHRIS Really? That good?

SARAH I didn't like the heroine. Too feisty.

CHRIS Feisty? What's wrong with feisty?

SARAH Every heroine's feisty these days. Why can't people write about bookish, gentle women?

CHRIS Cos they wouldn't sell any books.

SARAH I'd read them.

CHRIS What do you want me to get you next?

SARAH To read?

CHRIS Yeah.

SARAH Can you pick me up that last Austen? Probably about time I got round to it.

CHRIS OK. I'll pop into Waterstone's tomorrow.

SARAH Thanks, Chris. You're so good to me.

CHRIS I know.

Pause.

How's your eyesight? You said they were hurting last time you spent all day reading.

SARAH I was OK today, actually. Nice big print. But sooner or later I'm probably going to need one of those magnifying glasses. It'll have to be a large one. It's difficult enough turning the pages. But there's no way I'm getting a kindle! I need to smell books!

CHRIS I'll get you a magnifying glass tomorrow.

SARAH There's no rush.

CHRIS (*Pointedly*) I'll get you one tomorrow.

Pause.

SARAH I know you hate this.

CHRIS What?

SARAH Looking after me.

CHRIS No, Sarah.

SARAH I know you do. I can hear it in your voice. You're sick of me.

CHRIS Sarah, I love you. I'll do anything to make your life better for you.

SARAH I know but it's still a trial.

CHRIS You're my wife! I'll always make sure you're OK. I promise.

SARAH If you meant it you wouldn't need to promise.

CHRIS But I do. I promise. (*Beat*) I promised that I would look after you. Until one of us dies. And I meant it. So I'm here.

SARAH I know.

CHRIS Your imagination's been working too hard. I know it must be difficult spending all day with only your thoughts but I am yours. When I finish work and come home, I am yours. Please don't worry. You're always telling me not to.

SARAH I don't. I don't worry.

CHRIS No… Is there anything else I can get you? For during the day? To keep you occupied?

SARAH No, I'm fine. It's fine.

CHRIS You can have anything you want. Whatever you want, you can have it.

SARAH I'm fine.

Pause.

I hate being like this.

CHRIS Sarah, please, no, not again.

SARA I hate it, I hate it.

CHRIS Sarah.

SARAH You could never understand and I don't expect you to. But sometimes, when I'm sat here reading rubbish, and I can't even look out of the window, I just… Well, it gets me down.

CHRIS I know darling. It must be unbearable.

SARAH Sorry to go on. But I feel… I just feel like a bloody spa/stic.

CHRIS (*Immediately*) No, Sarah. Stop it. You're not. You are the most intelligent, vibrant, beautiful woman. I am so lucky to have even met you. I would do anything to keep you next to me.

SARAH Even like I am?

CHRIS You are still you.

SARAH Sometimes, it feels like I'm only half me.

Pause.

CHRIS Did you order the shopping with Tim for us?

SARAH Yeah, the delivery man put the things in the kitchen. There should be plenty.

CHRIS Well what do you want for dinner? I want to make us something gorgeous. Anything you like. What do you fancy? Entirely up to you.

SARAH Can we just have some soup, please? I'm not brilliantly hungry.

CHRIS *is disappointed. Pause.*

CHRIS (*He can't sound disappointed*) Soup it is. Any preference?

SARAH Just the first one out of the bag. Surprise me.

CHRIS (*Still disappointed*) OK sweetheart.

SARAH Thank you.

CHRIS What for?

SARAH Just for being here.

He looks at her. Some time. Then he heads into the kitchen.

Blackout.

SCENE 3

Some weeks later.

CHRIS *in bed with* **TAMMY**. *They've just had sex. Sweaty, deep breaths. Tired.*

CHRIS Fuck.

TAMMY (*Exhales loudly*) Oh God.

CHRIS Fuck.

TAMMY God.

CHRIS Fucking hell… Jesus.

They spend some time coming down, their breathing returning to normal.

CHRIS That was… amazing.

TAMMY Hmm.

CHRIS What? Wasn't it?

TAMMY No, it was good. It was good.

CHRIS Good?

TAMMY Yeah, no. It was really good.

CHRIS Well what was that then?

TAMMY What?

CHRIS That hmm. That little hmm you did.

TAMMY I didn't go hmm.

CHRIS You did. I said it was amazing. You went hmm.

TAMMY No I didn't.

CHRIS What you lying for? You went hmm. What's wrong?

TAMMY Nothing, nothing's wrong.

CHRIS What is it then? What was that fucking hmm about?

TAMMY There was no hmm.

CHRIS Right, stop it. You hmmed. Stop beating about the bush and just tell me what's on your mind. You've told me to enough times.

Pause.

TAMMY Well it's just…

CHRIS There we are. Knew it. Christ, go on then. What am I doing wrong?

TAMMY No, no. Nothing like that.

CHRIS What do you want me to do differently? Go on. What is it? I've heard it all before. Too fast, too slow, too short, what?

TAMMY (*For God's sake*) It's got nothing to do with your performance, you bloody paranoid.

CHRIS What then?

Long pause.

TAMMY Is this it?

CHRIS What do you mean?

TAMMY Is this all it's ever going to be is what I'm asking.

CHRIS Don't know what you mean.

TAMMY Well you're sat at home, you feel horny, you call me, I say yes?

CHRIS That's not how it is.

TAMMY Well that's how it bloody feels to me.

Pause.

CHRIS (*Realising*) Ah, I'm sorry. I'm sorry, Tammy. Come here…

He goes to hug her.

TAMMY No, I don't need a hug. A hug's no good, is it? I need you to grow a pair of bollocks man and make a decision.

Pause.

CHRIS Now listen, you knew. You *knew* my position way back when. You knew what you were signing up for.

TAMMY Right then. If that's how it is, I can't do it anymore.

CHRIS No, Tammy. I didn't mean it like…

TAMMY (*Interrupting*) Do you love your wife?

Pause.

CHRIS *is unsure whether to answer or not. Finally, he goes with her.*

CHRIS Yeah.

TAMMY Right.

CHRIS But I love you too. I do, I love you as well. Just as much.

TAMMY Well whoop-de-fucking-doo! You love me just as much, God I am blessed.

CHRIS No, look I didn't mean it like that, I meant...

TAMMY I know what you fucking mean.

Pause.

CHRIS (*Carefully*) You are helping me see what I need to do.

TAMMY And what does that mean?

CHRIS Tammy, please. I just need a little more time to...

TAMMY No, fucking hell. I am sat here waiting. Waiting to see if you ring or not. I can't make any plans, I can't go out, I can't... It's just shit actually. That's why I'm going fucking hmm in the bedroom. That's why. Cos this is shit and you are using me.

Pause.

CHRIS I'm sorry.

Pause.

I hate living with my wife.

TAMMY I don't want to know.

CHRIS And the only thing I hate about you is that you remind me of her.

Pause.

TAMMY You've obviously not known me long enough.

CHRIS I've known you six months.

TAMMY On and off. And only for this. Not to live with. Never long enough for me to properly irritate you.

CHRIS You wouldn't.

TAMMY And I bet you said the same to her once. 'No matter what happens, how bad you get, I'll be there. It won't irritate me one bit.'

Pause.

I can see how this is frightening you. I just want you to make your mind up.

CHRIS *sighs deeply.*

It must be horrible. And really scary. But I can't wait about in limbo. For you to dilly-dally. I need you to make a decision.

CHRIS I know you do.

TAMMY You need to make up your own mind. Cos I am getting tired of this shit. Why don't you go home and think about it for me?

CHRIS *stays lying next to her, staring at the ceiling.*

Blackout.

SCENE 4

CHRIS's living room.

He's just let on that he's playing around but not expanded.

SARAH Would you talk to me please? … Chris, would you please talk to me? … Chris, I need you to speak to me; I can't see you. Chris, please.

CHRIS What do you want me to say?

SARAH Just tell me. Tell me what's been going on.

CHRIS Sarah, it's difficult.

SARAH What, for you to open your mouth? To speak? I can't move, Chris. But I try. I use all my will and my strength just to move around the bungalow. I use everything I have in me, just to live ordinarily. And you can't open your mouth and speak?

CHRIS (*Vicious*) You're stuck here. How could you even begin to understand what it's like for me?

SARAH I've not *always* been here. I *know*!

Long pause.

CHRIS Course you do. I'm sorry. Sarah, I'm so sorry.

SARAH What for?

CHRIS For letting you go.

SARAH What does that mean?

CHRIS I left you a long time ago.

SARAH You're cheating on me?

CHRIS I left you a long time before that.

SARAH Endless bloody riddles. Would you just tell me what you mean?

CHRIS Yes.

SARAH Beg your pardon?

CHRIS Yes, I've been cheating on you.

Pause.

SARAH Well, I suspected as much. It had to happen.

CHRIS Sorry?

SARAH A man has needs, doesn't he? You need certain things and I can't give them to you. It was inevitable. I'm sorry, Chris. I'm sorry. I can't help it.

CHRIS (*Angry*) Don't apologise. Don't. Please, whatever you do, don't apologise. I couldn't bear that.

SARAH (*Strong, brave*) It's OK. I knew it would happen. In the end. I'm useless. Stuck like this.

CHRIS Stop it, Sarah. Stop it.

SARAH And I knew all along really. When did you ever go out with Steven when I was up and well?

CHRIS Sarah…

SARAH You started seeing *all* your old friends again. And they were all suddenly piss heads. You were out late…

CHRIS Sarah.

SARAH What does she look like?

CHRIS Sarah.

SARAH Please. You owe me one. What does she look like?

Pause.

CHRIS She looks like you… used to look.

SARAH Oh spare me.

CHRIS She does, she does, she does. She has the aspect of you.

SARAH You're a successful man. Moneyed. Why would she have to look like me? You're still sexy. She could look like anyone.

CHRIS She looks like you.

SARAH What's her name?

CHRIS No, Sarah, please.

SARAH Tell me.

CHRIS She's called Tamzin. Tammy.

SARAH Is Tammy your name for her?

CHRIS No. She hates Tamzin. Likes to be Tammy. I don't call her sweetheart, or darling, or love. She's Tammy. Just Tammy.

SARAH Did you meet her at work?

CHRIS Questions!

SARAH Come on. You might do me the courtesy of answering me.

CHRIS I met her in a bar. When I was out with Steven.

SARAH You met her at work.

CHRIS I didn't!

SARAH So you see her every day. She's always there.

CHRIS I met her in a bar, Sarah.

SARAH You'll be able to look up and see her whenever you like.

CHRIS Sarah, this is all in your head. You're going slowly mental.

Pause.

SARAH Are you in love with her?

CHRIS No. It's just sex.

SARAH Are you in love with her?

CHRIS No.

SARAH Are you in love with her?

Long pause.

Go to her then. Forget about me. Let Tim look after me. That's what he's paid to do. Sod off and be with her. You don't deserve this.

Pause.

Go then, Chris. You're wasting your life with me. Please. Go. Let me vegetate here.

Pause.

CHRIS But I love *you*.

SARAH Enough to sleep with somebody else?

CHRIS Sarah, this is an exceptional case. We can't… do it properly.

SARAH So it is just sex?

CHRIS Absolutely.

SARAH I don't believe you.

Pause.

I prepared myself for it, Chris. I'm just glad I got you for this long.

CHRIS Don't say things like that.

SARAH Why would you want to stay with me? You believe in romantic love. What's romantic about the way I am?

CHRIS You were my true love.

SARAH But not any more?

Pause.

CHRIS I don't think so, no.

Pause.

I can't leave you, Sarah.

SARAH Yes you can. You have *your* life to live. I can look after myself.

CHRIS You can't.

SARAH I have been.

CHRIS I've been here.

SARAH Not in spirit, Chris. I can't see your face but I know when you're lying. I know when you're upset. I know all the tiny, little nuances of expression. I can hear it in your voice and your teeth and your lips. I know that a long time ago, you abandoned me. Because I felt it. I heard it. And I'm not sad. I did know it wasn't going to last. How could it last?

Pause.

I'm sorry.

Pause.

CHRIS I love you.

SARAH (*Automatic*) I love you too.

Slow blackout. Nothing left to say.

SCENE 5

Park bench. Eating sandwiches.

TAMMY I don't think we've ever been out on a date before.

CHRIS Is this a date?

TAMMY You ask me to come to a park to "do lunch." Yeah, I'd say this were a date.

CHRIS We've *been* on a date.

TAMMY Eh?

CHRIS Trout special.

TAMMY If that's your idea of a date, I can see why we've been avoiding them.

CHRIS Yeah, I'm not very... I mean I can't actually remember when I last... Do you go on dates?

TAMMY I've done one or two in my time.

CHRIS Successful?

She looks witheringly at him.

Oh.

TAMMY Now you, Chris Whitworth give me an awful lot of bullshit but I'm pretty sure that when you do, you actually genuinely mean what you're saying. Other fellers give me bullshit because they're Grade A* prize-winning bullshitters.

CHRIS Guessing you've been with a lot of handsome guys?

TAMMY Trust me, the more handsome, the harder it is to trust 'em. The closer they are to scoring, the easier they lie to you.

CHRIS I'm not an habitual cheat, you know.

TAMMY I know. Well you couldn't be, could you?

CHRIS Hmm?

TAMMY Not handsome enough.

CHRIS I'm trying my best not to be insulted.

TAMMY So am I.

CHRIS How do you mean?

TAMMY Last time we were here. Out on a date. You wanted to give me bad news. I fear I am in for exactly the same right now.

CHRIS Well, no, it's not exactly...

TAMMY I am getting into a dangerous habit of asking you to bloody well spit it out.

CHRIS Yeah. Sorry.

TAMMY So will you just get on with it before I insert this prawn mayo somewhere.

CHRIS You asked me to think about things.

TAMMY Yeah.

CHRIS And I've thought about things.

TAMMY Right.

CHRIS I love my wife.

TAMMY Yeah.

CHRIS I love you.

TAMMY Yeah.

CHRIS And I still don't know what to do.

TAMMY (*Matter-of-fact*) Useless.

CHRIS So... I dunno... I've been thinking that... if I just... stopped seeing you then maybe it would all go away... and I could, you know, go home and try to get on with something.

Pause.

TAMMY Will she have you back?

CHRIS I'm not sure. I think maybe... in time...

TAMMY It's a risk.

CHRIS Please don't try and sway me.

TAMMY I'm not just. Just telling it like it is.

CHRIS OK.

TAMMY I reckon... despite whether you want to see me ever again or not... if you don't love your wife anymore, you should fucking leave her anyway.

Pause.

CHRIS You really are totally stone cold, aren't you?

TAMMY Pragmatic. It's no good for anyone not to be.

CHRIS Is this you telling people what they're doing's wrong and being helpful again?

TAMMY What do they expect, the idiots?! When it's so bloody obvious they can't see it.

CHRIS I'm not sure I like this side of you.

TAMMY I'm not sure I give much of a shit.

CHRIS Do you love me?

Pause.

TAMMY I don't know.

CHRIS No, then.

TAMMY No. I don't know.

CHRIS Right.

Pause.

I was happy, you know.

TAMMY I know you probably thought you were.

CHRIS What's that supposed to mean?

TAMMY You probably thought you were happy. I'm not sure you even thought about happiness at all, actually. I think you probably just lived a fairly vacuous life.

CHRIS Right. This analysing thing… It's… I think I'd like to go now.

TAMMY You just do whatever you want.

CHRIS I was happy, Tammy. I was… I thought I was.

TAMMY What's on your sandwich?

CHRIS Crab paste.

TAMMY Please don't be expecting a kiss.

Blackout.

SCENE 6

CHRIS's house.

CHRIS *has just entered. He has an empty box and some flowers.*

CHRIS It's only me.

SARAH What were you knocking for? No, wait, I can guess.

CHRIS I didn't want to wake you.

SARAH You've come to say goodbye.

CHRIS Sarah, please, let me do this my way.

SARAH I always have.

CHRIS Not fair.

SARAH No. Sorry.

Pause.

Well?

CHRIS I've been sleeping in a hotel.

SARAH Ha!

CHRIS I've been staying in a hotel!

SARAH What's it called?

CHRIS The hotel?

SARAH You've not been sleeping at a hotel.

CHRIS Sorry?

SARAH You hesitated.

Pause.

CHRIS I've been staying at the Gable Ends Hotel on Moor Street. It's a pink, dim room, with two bedside lamps, one of which doesn't work. It's got hangers attached to the wardrobe to stop people stealing them and the wardrobe isn't made of wood. It's a shitty thing with a metal frame, fitted plastic sheets around it and a zip up the middle. There's a faded painting of a little girl feeding ducks on the wall. It's fucking horrible and I'm paying far too much for it. I might as well be in a Travelodge.

Pause.

SARAH What, and that's your penance is it?

CHRIS Where do you want me to go?

SARAH I want you to be yourself man!

CHRIS I have been! Too much! Evidently!

SARAH Just be you, Chris. Just be *you*. Cos I think you're marvellous and I…

SARAH *starts crying beneath her head of hair. We hear her sniffles.* **CHRIS** *stands, unable to say anything.*

Ignore me. Sorry. (*She sniffs.*)

CHRIS Do you need me to get you a hankie?

SARAH No, I'll be fine. I don't need anything.

CHRIS Don't be like this. I didn't mean… Sarah… Please don't torture me for this.

SARAH (*Shouts*) What do you think you've put me through you bastard!

CHRIS Do you not think my guilt is punishment enough, Sarah?

SARAH No.

Pause.

CHRIS I brought a box. I assumed you'd want me out. I've come to pick up a few things. You can have whatever you want. Keep anything.

SARAH That's very gracious of you.

CHRIS Sarah.

SARAH Sorry. I just… can't keep being kind.

Pause.

CHRIS I'll just take what I need then. The rest is yours.

SARAH Do it another time.

CHRIS I need some clothes. I need my toothbrush, that sort of stuff.

SARAH Take what you immediately need, and come for the rest another time. I can't have you around here tonight. It's too hard.

Pause.

CHRIS Thing is I'm not coming back. After tonight. That's it. I've got money. I'm going away.

SARAH You're not going to Tammy's?

CHRIS I *do* need to be me. You're right. I need to find out who I am again. So I'm going to go away. I need my essentials and nothing else. You can have everything. If you want to get divorced send me a letter. I'll let you know where I'm staying through the post so you'll have an address. And I'll send you whatever money you want. For the rest of your life if you want it. I'll always support you, Sarah.

SARAH I can get enough love and money from the council, thanks.

CHRIS (*Softly, desperate, faltering*) Then I'll send you some books.

Pause.

SARAH Your taste in books was not the reason I married you, Chris.

CHRIS You mean…

SARAH Every book you ever chose for me…

CHRIS You never said.

SARAH Didn't want to hurt you.

Pause.

CHRIS And my collection? What did you make of that?

SARAH (*Deprecatingly*) A collection of first edition Stephen King novels?

Pause.

Do I have to say it?

Pause.

CHRIS Well that last one you bought me didn't even have a fucking dust jacket, did it? It was totally useless!

Pause. Then they both start laughing sadly.

I'll put these flowers in a vase for you. They'll be good for a week at least. They were expensive.

SARAH Do you want me to see them wilting? Take them with you.

Pause.

CHRIS Has Tim been round?

SARAH Yes. Lots. And Irene from up the street. She's a funny old lady.

CHRIS So you've got company?

SARAH Yep.

Pause.

CHRIS I can probably buy a toothbrush.

SARAH I'll miss you, Chris.

Pause.

CHRIS *goes over to* **SARAH** *and lifts her head. She protests.*

No, Chris. Stop/it. Stop it. Please. Chris.

CHRIS *tilts her so that we can see her face.*

CHRIS You're gonna see me when I say this. Don't look away, Sarah Whitworth. (*And she's stopped talking over him.*) I love you. And even yet, you remain the most beautiful woman in the world.

CHRIS *kisses* **SARAH**. *A long kiss like a 50's movie. She struggles against it but hasn't the strength to stop him.*

He replaces her head so that she is again looking into her lap and her face is gone. He picks up the flowers and the box.

CHRIS That's it.

Snap blackout.

EPILOGUE

CHRIS *in same lighting state as* PROLOGUE.

CHRIS There comes a point when you think you've cracked life. And then it all just goes mad. And that's how it sort of... went. Painful, protracted. Longer than it needed to be. But... equally... it felt stimulating, new, like an adventure I wasn't in control of. (*Suddenly he's not addressing the audience*) Can you see why we never spoke about her? Why I was so guarded when it came to talking about her?

Enter **TAMMY**.

TAMMY I'm still not completely sure. To be honest.

CHRIS What did you expect me to say, Tammy? "You know something, you look just like my wife. Shall we go on a date?" You'd've run a mile.

TAMMY Yes, course. Sorry.

CHRIS And *if* I'd told you. If you'd known. From the start. Then it wouldn't have been my choice. To leave her. It'd've been *ours*. Cos you'd have been involved then. So please don't mention her again. We don't have to think about her. Ever again.

TAMMY I thought...

CHRIS Shush. Just, please, Tammy. Can we not just leave her alone now?

TAMMY Course we can my love.

She kisses him on the cheek. They hug so that they can't see each other's faces.

TAMMY Do you *still* see her in me?

Long pause.

CHRIS No.

Blackout.

End.

NOTES FROM THE AUTHOR

Hylton Collins wanted to perform in *Trigonometry* since he first read it six years ago. He fancied himself as a bit of a Lothario, you see? He's been reading my scripts since I was at University and we've been doing readings and productions together ever since.

After *Answering to the Governor* at the Lowry Studio, we embarked on our first production for the GM Fringe; *Hardwired*. I dare say it was received very enthusiastically by our wonderful audience at The Swan. Being involved in the Fringe was a terrific experience and we knew we wanted to do more.

Hylton persisted with the belief that *Trigonometry* deserved a second life after its rehearsed reading at the 24:7 Festival and it was rewritten as a two-act play in a much tighter, more streamlined form, with the extra years of experience helping me realize what needed cutting, editing and binning.

Winning the Best New Writing Prize through WFTS was a massive surprise and I have Hylton to thank for helping the play find its final form. It's such a lovely thing to get a vote of confidence as a writer because you never quite know if what you've written is actually any good. This award means an awful lot to me.

John FK Hoyle. July 2016.

ABOUT THE AUTHOR

John was born and grew up in Shaw, Oldham and became involved in local amateur theatre in his teens at Playhouse 2. He continues to support the theatre, making appearances as an actor and directing.

John read English and Related Literature at The University of York. He appeared at The National Student Drama Festival twice in productions of *Gagarin Way* and *Stone Cold, Dead Serious* with the York University Drama Society.

He now works as a Primary School teacher in Middleton and lives with his fiancée, her two children and his Doctor Who collection.

His other performed work includes:

Answering to the Governor, The Lowry Studio Theatre

Hardwired, JHC Productions and The Swan

NOTES FROM THE PUBLISHER

Studio Salford has been around since 2003 and is a collective of in-house theatre companies producing new work in the intimate spaces at The Kings Arms Theatre. Through its productions, Development Week and development night (*Embryo*) many writers, actors and directors have learnt the ropes and have gone onto big things.

Mike Heath runs the *Studio Salford WriteForTheStage* (WFTS) courses, supported by Arts Council England. WFTS has been running since 2010 and has helped developed over 20 full length stage-play and over 35 short pieces. Work produced through the courses have gone on to full productions with (and without) support from Arts Council England. Participant writers have gone onto to full rural touring of subsequent work and publication of novels.

WFTS is based at The Kings Arms, Salford but is also available for distance learning. Details of the course can be found at **www.writeforthestage.co.uk**

WriteForTheStage Books is the publishing arm of the WFTS courses. The aim is to help sustain the life of the work produced through the course once the course has been completed. More information is available on the website.

PERFORM THIS PLAY

The following rights are available for this play:

Professional Rights
Amateur Rights
Fringe Rights
Educational Rights

To find out how to get the rights to perform this play in part or in full, please email **info@writeforthestage.co.uk**

BE A PLAYWRIGHT

Do you dream of seeing your writing on stage, performed by professional actors and in front of an audience? Maybe you don't know where to start.

The *Studio Salford WriteForTheStage* courses cater for total beginners, learning the fundamentals of story-telling for the stage, to more experienced writers who require guidance and dramaturgy support.

Supported by Arts Council England, *WriteForTheStage* is an affordable means of learning and developing your skills. Based in Salford, Greater Manchester, Glossop and online, there's a course that will help you onto the next stage of your career.

See **www.writeforthestage.co.uk** for more details.

60097575R00054

Made in the USA
Charleston, SC
21 August 2016